W9-BPS-350

Monet Paints a Day

Julie Danneberg

Illustrated by Caitlin Heimerl

Charlesbridge

DiPietro Library
Franklin Pierce University
Rindge, NH 03461

To Walker, Alex, and Jack
and our perfect day at Giverny
—J. D.

For Mom, Dad, and Drew,

with love—C. H.

Text copyright © 2012 by Julie Danneberg
Illustrations copyright © 2012 by Caitlin Heimerl
All rights reserved, including the right of reproduction in
whole or in part in any form. Charlesbridge and colophon
are registered trademarks of Charlesbridge Publishing, Inc.

Published by Charlesbridge
85 Main Street
Watertown, MA 02472
(617) 926-0329
www.charlesbridge.com

Library of Congress Cataloging-in-Publication Data
Danneberg, Julie, 1958–
    Monet paints a day / Julie Danneberg; illustrated by Caitlin Heimerl.
        p. cm.
    ISBN 978-1-58089-240-7 (reinforced for library use)
    ISBN 978-1-60734-454-4 (ebook pdf)
1. Monet, Claude, 1840–1926—Juvenile literature. I. Monet, Claude,
1840–1926. II. Heimerl, Caitlin. III. Title.
ND553.M7D36   2012
759.4—dc23   2011025789

Printed in China
(hc) 10 9 8 7 6 5 4 3

Illustrations done in watercolor on Arches paper
Display type and letters set in P22 Monet, based on Monet's handwriting
    and text type set in Goudy
Color separations by KHL Chroma Graphics, Singapore
Printed by Imago in China
Production supervision by Brian G. Walker
Designed by Susan Mallory Sherman

November 1885

Dear Alice,

This morning I went under the Manneporte to paint. I want to make a success of it because it's very beautiful, but very difficult I think.

I, Claude Monet, Impressionist painter, step out of the Hotel Blanquet ready to paint the day.

Winter sunlight pours through the sparkling morning mist, and a gaggle of children wait for me, anxious to carry my half-finished paintings. Like a string of ducklings, they follow me, toting my canvases while I carry my paint box and palette.

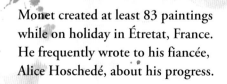

Monet created at least 83 paintings
while on holiday in Étretat, France.
He frequently wrote to his fiancée,
Alice Hoschedé, about his progress.

Carefully, we make our way down the zigzagging cliff path
and then trudge across the rocky beach.

Most of the painters during Monet's
time made sketches outside and then
returned to their studios to paint.
Monet preferred to paint nature right
on the spot, even though it meant
lugging all his equipment and supplies
to and from the hotel every day.

When we finally reach the crescent-shaped strip of sand, surrounded by towering cliffs, I stop. "We are here," I say. The children carefully set down my canvases. I toss them candy and coins, and then they scatter like seagulls. They know that I can be sunny and pleasant one minute and then, suddenly, my anger can roll in like a storm cloud. What makes me angry? Bad weather, poor light, and most of all, frustration with my painting.

Monet's frustration sometimes led to temper tantrums. When he was angry he might throw paintings he disliked into the water or rip them apart, and once he even burned some that especially displeased him.

I turn to study the water.

Before me stretches the endlessly moving sea.

Above me looms the unchanging stone arch called
the Manneporte.

Around me swirls the shimmering, golden sunlight.

Impressionists tried to capture
the feeling, or impression, of a
scene rather than an exact copy.
To do this they used lighter,
brighter colors and quick
brushstrokes.

Flipping through my unfinished canvases, I choose one that matches today's glittering morning. I unfold my easel and stool, and prepare my palette.

The wind spatters sand against my neck and into my paints, but I don't mind. I concentrate on mixing the paint colors to capture the pinks and oranges of the stone arch, the blues and violets of the horizon, and the greens of the rolling waves.

Monet often had with him several partially finished paintings of the same scene. As time passed and the light changed, he would move to a different canvas, choosing one that matched the time of day, weather, and light in front of him.

Quickly I . . .

ruffle my paintbrush against the canvas as jade waters

   ruffle against the shore's edge . . .

drag paint across the canvas as retreating waves

   drag silver sand into the ocean . . .

flutter and dab my brush at the canvas as the sea foam

   flutters briefly above the surf and disappears.

Monet painted at a feverish pace, feeling that he had only about 7 to 15 minutes to work on a painting before the light changed and he had to switch to another one.

Monet later told Alice that although he had noticed the waves at his feet, he thought the tide was going out, not coming in.

The rumbling waves explode a warning at my feet, but I can't stop painting. Not now. "Faster, faster, only a few more minutes to catch this light," I mutter to myself.

Swoosh.

A giant wave towers over me.

Swish.

It knocks me down.

Crash.

Water rains down
over my head,
over my easel,
over my painting.

The wave drags me into the sea, which swallows me whole.
I tumble like a shell against the bottom of the ocean.
My lungs empty, and my heart pounds with fear. I look
desperately toward the surface.

And then the ocean spits me out. My heart swells with relief. I lie on the sand, gasping for breath, still clinging to my palette. Wiping away bits of cadmium yellow and cobalt blue paint stuck in my beard, I look around for my easel, my stool, my painting. . . . Alas, everything is gone. Taken by the glistening green waves.

The cause of all this, as I never go out without checking the exact hour of the tide, is that, having seen the agenda in the hotel which gives the times of the tides, I didn't notice that yesterday's sheet hadn't been torn off.

The worst of it is that I lost my broken canvas.

Nature is greatness, power, and immortality.

I trudge away from the crescent-shaped beach. Away from the stone arch. Across the rocks. Up the zigzagging path. Toward the hotel, where dry clothes, a warm fire, and a soothing cup of tea await.

As I reach the top of the cliff, I face the sea one more time, knowing that I will be back again tomorrow.

Author's Note

Claude Monet (1840–1926) was one of a group of French painters known as the Impressionists. Before these artists came along, traditional painters believed that art was meant to teach or inspire. They worked in studios where they painted detailed, lifelike scenes from the Bible or from mythology. Traditional painters spent a great deal of time composing and sketching before they painted. They generally used dark, somber colors in their work.

The Impressionists had a new approach. They painted images from the real world—pictures of diners at restaurants and ballet dancers, street scenes and steaming trains pulling into stations. Using bold, bright colors, they captured the feeling—or *impression*—of what they saw rather than the exact details. They used the thickness of the paint and brash brushstrokes, in addition to color, to help communicate their impressions.

Unfortunately, the first time critics and the public saw the Impressionists' work, they said their paintings were so ugly they could cause stomach upset. Undaunted, the Impressionists organized their own art shows. Slowly the public and the critics changed their minds and began to enjoy the lighter, brighter work.

Today Monet's paintings can be found in museums all over the world, and they are worth millions of dollars.

The events in *Monet Paints a Day* took place in November of 1885. The forty-five-year-old painter was on an extended painting trip to Étretat, France, a well-known seaside resort and fishing village located along the English Channel. This expedition went as many had before. He rose early, painted all day, and then returned to the hotel for a sociable dinner with the other guests. After dinner he read, wrote letters, and prepared to do it all again the next day.

When I wrote this book, I intended the story to read in much the same way as one might view Monet's Impressionist paintings. Although you don't see all the details of Monet's life and art in this story, you certainly get a sense of how single-minded and focused Monet was when he worked. He spent a lifetime trying to capture on canvas the beauty of nature, of light, of air, and of water. Just as one of Monet's paintings showed his feelings or impressions of a particular moment in time, so this story shows an impression of a day in Claude Monet's extended life as a painter, a career that lasted more than sixty years and produced more than two thousand paintings.

Waves at the Manneporte, 1885. Courtesy of
North Carolina Museum of Art, promised gift
of Dr. and Mrs. James H. Goodnight

Monet's Painting Techniques

Monet worked as a painter for more than fifty years, his style growing and changing throughout his career. During the time he was in Étretat, there were certain art supplies and painting techniques he consistently employed.

Monet ordered paints and supplies from an art dealer in Paris, who then shipped him whatever he needed whenever he needed it. Improvements in paints and supplies during the mid-nineteenth century made it easier for artists, such as Monet, to paint away from their studios. *Canvas*

stretched across a wooden frame was more lightweight to carry than the previously used wooden panels. The canvases Monet used were *pre-primed* with an undercoating of pale or light colors, so when he started a new painting, he wasn't setting paint to a bare canvas. This approach served two purposes. The primer coat formed a protective

surface between the paint and the canvas, and it also kept the canvas from rotting. After 1840 *oil paints* came in tin tubes, much better than the pig bladders of old, which were easily damaged.

Monet and other artists from this period usually carried

a *kit,* which was a wooden box containing their favorite paints, a bundle of different types of *brushes,* and a *palette.* The word *palette* refers both to a wooden platelike object on which painters squeezed out

and mixed paints, and to the preferred colors that painters used in their paintings (Monet limited his palette to eight or nine colors). When squeezed from the tube, oil paint has the consistency of toothpaste. Depending on the effect and the color Monet wanted to create, he had various ways of getting the paint onto the canvas. He might squirt the oil

paint onto his palette, and then change its texture by mixing in a little more oil, blotting out the extra oil, or even adding a touch of turpentine to thin it out. He might put several colors on his palette, then take a dip of this and a dab of that, mixing them together to make new colors. Sometimes, though, he would just load his brush with "straight" color from his palette, or the tube, and mix that paint into paint already on his canvas. Other times he obtained color by putting two straight colors next to each other on the canvas, say yellow and blue, knowing that viewers' eyes would mix the colors in their heads and see green.

Although Monet didn't make detailed sketches of his paintings, neither did he sit down in front of

a scene, or *motif* as he called it, and just begin painting. Any scene that he chose to paint had previously been scouted out and decided upon after much thought about its composition, or arrangement.

Georges Jeanniot, a journalist who watched Monet paint during the late 1880s, said that once the painter was in front of his canvas he drew in a few *charcoal* lines and then began to paint. Monet filled the canvas quickly, later returning, time and again, to add details of light and color.

Looking at his paintings, though, we can see that, whatever technique he used, his art was alive with movement, light, and color.

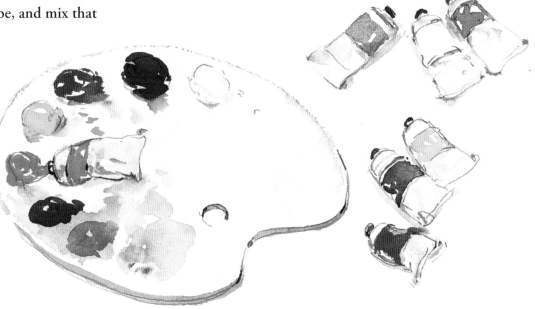

Bibliography

Candlish, Louise and Fergus Day, eds. *Art Book: Monet.* New York: Dorling Kindersley, 1999.

Connolly, Sean. *Claude Monet.* Milwaukee, WI: World Almanac Library, 2005.

Copplestone, Trewin. *Claude Monet.* New York: Regency House Publishing, 1998.

Forge, Andrew. *Monet.* Chicago: The Art Institute of Chicago, 1995.

Mason, Antony. *Famous Artists: Monet.* New York: Barron's, 1995.

Morgan, Genevieve, ed. *Monet: The Artist Speaks.* San Francisco: Collins Publishers, 1996.

Morris, Catherine. *The Essential Claude Monet.* New York: Harry N. Abrams, Inc., 1999.

Muhlburger, Richard. *What Makes a Monet a Monet?* New York: The Metropolitan Museum of Art, 1993.

Rachman, Carla. *Monet A& I (Art and Ideas).* London: Phaidon Press Limited, 1997.

Russell, Vivian. *Monet's Landscapes.* Boston: Little, Brown and Co., 2000.

Spate, Virgina. *Claude Monet: Life and Work.* New York: Rizzoli, 1992.

Taillandier, Yvon. *Monet.* New York: Crown Publishers, Inc., 1993.

Tucker, Paul Hayes. *Claude Monet: Life and Art.* New Haven: Yale University Press, 1995.

Waldron, Ann. *First Impressions: Claude Monet.* New York: Harry N. Abrams, Inc., 1999.

Welton, Jude. *Monet.* New York: Dorling Kindersley in association with the Musée Marmottan, Paris, 1992.

Franklin Pierce University

00216925